THIS CANDLEWICK BIOGRAPHY BELONGS TO:

THE SECRET WORLD OF
Walter Anderson

Hester Bass ILLUSTRATED BY *E. B. Lewis*

CANDLEWICK PRESS

To Clayton, who shares the journey.
With gratitude to Fairy Godmother Rosemary, Princess Liz, and Duke Earl.
And a thousand flowers to Paul, the Prince of Serendipity.
H. B.

To the victims of Hurricane Katrina
E. B. L.

TABLE OF CONTENTS

CHAPTER ONE

There once was a man whose love of nature was as wide as the world.

There once was an artist who needed to paint as much as he needed to breathe.

There once was an islander who lived in a cottage at the edge of Mississippi, where the sea meets the earth and the sky.

His name was Walter Anderson.

He may be the most famous American artist you've never heard of.

To see a green heron's nest, he would climb a tree.
To draw a sphinx moth against a pattern of bullrushes,
he would wade up to his shoulders.

Art was an adventure, and Walter Anderson
was an explorer, first class.

While the sun was still sleeping, Walter Anderson would get ready for a trip to his favorite place to paint. He used metal garbage cans as suitcases. He packed apples and raisins and peanut butter and rice. He packed paints and brushes and pencils and 8½ x 11 inch typing paper.

He wore his scruffy old weather-beaten hat.

He never went anywhere without his hat. It shaded his eyes, held art supplies, and often transported his models, such as snakes, birds, and raccoons.

CHAPTER TWO

Walter locked the door to one little room in his cottage. He didn't let anybody in there — maybe a possum or a mouse, but not his wife or his children.

Nobody. Ever. That was *his* little room.

He pinned a note to the screen door of his front porch: Gone to Horn Island. A star was still shining in the sky, and cricket song hung in the air.

Walter had found pieces of a boat washed up on the beach and put them back together like a puzzle. He slid this leaky green skiff into the bayou that led to Biloxi Bay, which led to the Mississippi Sound and the Gulf of Mexico beyond.

A kingfisher rattled farewell. A blue heron stood at attention.

There were twelve miles of open water between Ocean Springs, Mississippi, and Horn Island. Sometimes Walter used an umbrella for a sail, but usually he rowed every stroke.

Dolphins and pelicans escorted Walter on his journey. The sun and the wind and his shadow kept him company. His boat bobbed in the waves for hours and hours until he pulled the skiff onshore.

There would be no warm bed waiting for Walter. No running water. No bathroom or kitchen. Horn was a wild, windswept barrier island, where life had never been easy. Once there had been a lighthouse. Once there had been a farm. But no one lived on Horn Island anymore.

There were biting flies, hungry mosquitoes, swarming gnats, fire ants, venomous snakes, blistering heat, blinding sun, freezing cold, stinging rain, and roaring wind. But for Walter, to paint on Horn Island was to be in paradise.

CHAPTER THREE

Walter was not alone on Horn Island. He had many friends there. After he set up camp, Walter sometimes held a housewarming banquet, with prunes for the raccoons and rice for the rabbits and birds. The rats always got some, too.

When Walter was thirsty, he got fresh water from an old well he called Rabbit Springs. When it went brackish, wild hogs left over from the farm helped him find water to drink.

Walter would stay on Horn Island for weeks at a time, in all kinds of weather, using his boat as a shelter.

When Walter was hungry, he often had a mystery feast, because the cans of food he brought would get wet and the labels would slide off.

He cooked over a fire. Sometimes he would eat whatever washed up. A jar of pickles, an orange — there was always something on the beach.

Once there were seven or eight miles of bananas!
Food was scarce on the island, and the animals seemed
to dance around all those bananas on the sand.
    And Walter painted them.

CHAPTER FOUR

Walter also kept journals, writing and drawing about everything he experienced. He called them logs, and they reveal how deeply he wanted to harmonize with the symphony of nature.

Walter would draw and paint all his friends on Horn Island from sunrise till after nightfall. He especially loved that last magic hour before sunset, as the colors of the world were melting into darkness.

Sometimes he got animals to come closer by feeding them like pets. Reddy the duck. Split-Ear the rabbit. Inky the raccoon. Slimy the frog.

Sometimes Walter tried to rescue animals, but often they were too sick or hurt to be saved. He would paint them even in death, for they were still magnificent and because images were food for Walter Anderson, and on an island, no food is ever wasted.

Some people called him crazy for living like a hermit just to paint fish and animals and birds and plants. But Walter Anderson spent some of the happiest times of his life on Horn Island.

CHAPTER FIVE

Walter Anderson survived snakebite and hurricanes, but in 1965, he became seriously ill. Nevertheless, he continued drawing. While in the hospital, he drew the other patients. Doctors did everything that could be done, but Walter Anderson died in the city of New Orleans, where he had been born sixty-two years before.

The little room in his cottage was still locked.

What was inside remained a mystery.

Until one day, his wife unlocked the door, and what she saw took her breath away.

The walls were covered with paintings of a Gulf Coast day. Animals creeping home at dawn. Birds roosting in the trees at sunset. All crowned by a giant zinnia on the ceiling.

There was art everywhere.

Throughout his life, he had painted murals and block prints and pottery for everybody else, for the public. But Walter Anderson had kept his Horn Island paintings and drawings private, hidden, just for himself.

Walter Anderson took the time to truly see what was all around him. He concentrated so intensely on his subjects that he felt he became that tree, that flower, or that bird— especially among his friends on Horn Island.

He painted because that's what he loved to do. He saw the world in a wildly original way, and he transformed his experience into shapes and lines, patterns and colors.

Walter Anderson painted to realize his secret world, to bring himself and nature into one thing called art.

Pine Trees and Dunes, 1960. Watercolor on paper, 8½ x 11 in.

AUTHOR'S NOTE

Best known for his Horn Island watercolors, Walter Anderson was a skilled and prolific artist who also created oil paintings, drawings, decorated ceramics, wood sculpture, block prints, murals, poetry, and prose. He has been called a mad genius and a homegrown van Gogh.

Born in New Orleans in 1903, Walter Anderson grew up surrounded by books and birds, art and animals, and bookend brothers destined to become artists, too. He was an enthusiastic reader, favoring mythology, folklore, history, science, music, and art.

The boys' mother was artistic and made sure they followed in her footsteps. Their businessman father made sure they could make a living at it.

Walter, who was nicknamed Bob, spent the 1920s studying art, first at what would become Parsons The New School for Design in New York, then graduating from the Pennsylvania Academy of the Fine Arts in Philadelphia.

At the Academy, he sometimes grew tired of the classroom and escaped to the zoo to draw animals from life. His drawings of lions, bears, and monkeys won the Packard Prize. He later won a Cresson scholarship to study in France.

Walter saw the great museums in Paris but spent most of his time on foot or on a bicycle, seeing the countryside and admiring the cathedrals. He was most impressed by prehistoric cave paintings in the south of France. Flickering images of ancient animals, seen by torchlight, burned in his mind.

Walter returned home from school on the eve of the Depression. The Andersons had left New Orleans and moved to more than twenty acres of wild Mississippi coastline in Ocean Springs. They called it Shearwater.

His older brother, Peter, founded the family business of Shearwater Pottery in 1928 and became a master potter, creating utilitarian ware of simple beauty, prized for its distinctive glazes and shapes. Walter decorated Peter's vases, bowls, and plates with animals, birds, people, flowers, and geometry. He was greatly influenced by the idea of seven artistic motifs composed of lines and curves, as described by Mexican artist Best-Maugard.

Walter and his younger brother, Mac, made and decorated what they called widgets and gadgets — figurines of pirates, athletes, and fairy-tale characters as well as creatures from the yard and the bayou — inspired by literature, their surroundings, and their imagination.

Walter decorated ten pieces of pottery a week for ten dollars. He finally made enough money to marry Agnes Grinstead, nicknamed Sissy, in 1933. They moved into the cottage at Shearwater. He hooked rugs, block-printed curtains, and built most of the furniture, including a chair carved to resemble a pelican and a table supported by sculpted blue jays.

In 1935, Walter Anderson painted murals for Ocean Springs High School: Native Americans hunting deer, local fishermen catching mullet. He was making a living as an artist in the 1930s, when it was hard to make a living at all.

But in 1937, Walter Anderson became ill. His mind was tortured. He escaped one hospital and walked home, following railroad tracks for a thousand miles. He escaped another hospital by tying bed sheets together. As he slid down a brick wall, he used a bar of soap to draw birds, flying away with him.

His doctors said he needed rest. Walter felt he needed more time to paint.

In 1940, the Walter Andersons moved to nearby Gautier to live at Oldfields, Sissy's father's rambling waterfront home. Making art did make Walter better.

Walter Anderson made a calendar of drawings—one a day—for more than three years. He made puppets, toys, and books for his children. He used crayons to create astonishingly sophisticated drawings. He explored rivers, bayous, and islands. He took long bicycle trips and made maps of his journeys.

Above left: *Lion*, 1924. Charcoal on paper, 9 x 11¾ in.
Right: *Chesty Horse*, 1935. Ceramic, 13½ x 4½ x 14 in.

Walter carved images from myths, fairy tales, and life on the Gulf Coast on huge blocks of linoleum, in reverse, then printed the pictures on the back of old wallpaper. He wanted everyone to be able to afford to bring art into their homes, so he charged only one dollar per foot for intricate block prints.

Walter read book after book at night by lamplight. He turned the pages with his left hand while his right hand dipped a pen in ink and drew pictures inspired by the words. By morning, drawings covered the floor like fallen leaves.

But the everyday stresses of family life were too much for Walter to bear.

In 1946, before his fourth child was born, Walter went back to the cottage at Shearwater. His wife and children eventually followed, but they would never all live in the same house again.

Walter's family lived in a converted barn across the path from the cottage. Walter's very survival seemed to depend on working alone, and although the separation was very painful, his family loved him enough to let him.

In Ocean Springs, everybody knew that crazy artist who rode his bicycle everywhere. In 1950, when the city was building a new community center, Walter Anderson offered to

paint murals on the ninety-foot walls as a gift, yet the city contracted to pay him one dollar.

Above: *Thumbelina*, 1945. Linocut on paper, 24 x 61 in.
Left: *Cottage*, 1948–1950. Watercolor on paper, 8½ x 11 in.

He spent one year painting the arrival of French and French-Canadian explorers in 1699 greeted by Native Americans and accurately depicted the plants and animals of the Gulf Coast. The mural is considered his masterpiece today, but at the time, people were not ready for his generosity. Some townspeople didn't like it and wanted to paint over it. Walter never cashed the one-dollar check. He could find no peace on the mainland, so he sought it elsewhere.

Ocean Springs Community Center Mural, detail, c. 1950. Oil and tempera on stucco

Walter began to spend more and more time on Horn Island—his refuge, his heaven, his salvation. He wrote volume after volume of logs—full of observations, poetry, and drawings—chronicling his many journeys there. And he painted watercolors.

In September 1965, Walter Anderson survived Hurricane Betsy by tying himself to his boat and experiencing the storm from the highest dune on Horn Island. Two months later, he died following an operation for lung cancer at age sixty-two.

In 1991, just before Sissy's death, a museum was established in Ocean Springs to showcase Walter Anderson's art. Storms and humidity threatened the Little Room in the cottage, so it was moved to safety within the museum. Walter's rickety skiff, his rusted bicycle, and his battered old hat are often on display.

In 2003, to celebrate what would have been his one hundredth birthday, the Smithsonian Institution in Washington, D.C., honored Walter Anderson with an exhibition of his life's work called "Everything I See Is New and Strange."

Self Portrait, 1960. Watercolor on paper, 11 x 8½ in.

Thousands of people saw his art, many for the first time, and marveled at its depth and variety. He was called an American master.

As one of the oldest continuously operating art potteries in the United States, Shearwater attracted people from all over the world. It seemed to be a magical place. People felt a change in atmosphere and quality of light as soon as they crossed the paved street onto the unpaved roads of the property.

Time appeared to stand still at Shearwater, as if the past, present, and future were inseparably one. Some of the weathered buildings had stood since the 1830s and looked much the same as when Walter Anderson lived and worked there.

Then came August 29, 2005, and Hurricane Katrina.

A storm surge estimated at up to twenty-eight feet crashed ashore at Shearwater and took much of the legacy of the Anderson family out to sea.

The people evacuated and survived, but sixteen buildings were damaged or destroyed, including nine family homes. The destructive power of nature was fearsomely displayed. Debris was piled high.

The pottery showroom and workrooms were gutted. The Walter Anderson family vault, containing their personal collection, was flooded with six feet of water. Walter's cottage was knocked off its foundation and devastated. The artwork at the museum in downtown Ocean Springs, farther from the coastline, was thankfully safe. But much of this cultural heritage was damaged or lost forever.

Nevertheless, the Anderson family has deep roots at Shearwater and, like the live oaks that endured the storm, they have resolved to stand sure. The pottery has been rebuilt, the cottage has been righted but needs repair, and nature has revealed its

Blue Jays, c. 1960. Watercolor on paper, 8½ x 11 in.

equally remarkable ability to heal.

My admiration for Walter Anderson began when I was introduced to his work in the early 1980s. Providence sent my family to live in Ocean Springs in 1996, when my husband, Clayton Bass, became the executive director of the Walter Anderson Museum of Art. For the next seven years, I had the privilege to visit Horn Island—now protected as part of the Gulf Islands National Seashore—and to savor all the art that the entire Anderson family created. These treasures of the Gulf Coast must be preserved for future generations.

A portion of my proceeds from this book will be donated to the families of the three Anderson brothers—Peter, Walter, and Mac—and to the Walter Anderson Museum of Art, to support their efforts to conserve the artwork that can be saved.

For many, Walter Anderson's work speaks of the hope and renewal to be found in nature, the interconnectedness of all life, and the importance of art in our lives. Such a message is eternal and will survive any storm, just like Horn Island.

Horn Island, c. 1960. Watercolor on paper, three separate sheets, each 8½ x 11 in.

SELECTED BIBLIOGRAPHY

For Children:

Anderson, Walter. *An Alphabet.* Jackson, MS: University Press of Mississippi, 1984/1992.

———. *Robinson: The Pleasant History of an Unusual Cat.* Jackson, MS: University Press of Mississippi, 1982.

Douglas, Ellen. *The Magic Carpet and Other Tales.* Illustrated by Walter Anderson. Jackson, MS: University Press of Mississippi, 1987.

Morrison, Ann, and Patti Black, eds. *Walter Anderson for Children.* Jackson, MS: Mississippi Department of Archives and History, 1984. Reprint, Ocean Springs, MS: Walter Anderson Museum of Art, 1992.

Walter Anderson's Art:

Anderson, Walter. *Birds.* Jackson, MS: University Press of Mississippi, 1990.

———. *A Symphony of Animals.* Jackson, MS: University Press of Mississippi, 1996.

King, Anne R. *Walls of Light: The Murals of Walter Anderson.* Jackson, MS: University Press of Mississippi and Walter Anderson Museum of Art, 1999.

Pickard, Mary Anderson, and Patricia Pinson, eds. *Form and Fantasy: The Block Prints of Walter Anderson.* Jackson, MS: University Press of Mississippi, 2007.

Pinson, Patricia, ed. *The Art of Walter Anderson.* Jackson, MS: University Press of Mississippi and the Walter Anderson Museum of Art, 2003.

Stewart, Dod with Marjorie Anderson Ashley and Earl Lamar Denham. *Shearwater Pottery.* Slidell, LA: Bristol Publishing, 2005.

Sugg, Redding S. Jr. *A Painter's Psalm: The Mural from Walter Anderson's Cottage.* Jackson, MS: University Press of Mississippi, 1992.

For Adults:

Anderson, Agnes Grinstead. *Approaching the Magic Hour: Memories of Walter Anderson.* Jackson, MS: University Press of Mississippi, 1989/1995.

Anderson, Leif. *Dancing with My Father.* Jackson, MS: University Press of Mississippi, 2005.

Maurer, Christopher. *Fortune's Favorite Child: The Uneasy Life of Walter Anderson.* Jackson, MS: University Press of Mississippi, 2003.

——— with Maria Estrella Iglesias. *Dreaming in Clay on the Coast of Mississippi.* New York: Doubleday, 2000.

Sugg, Redding S. Jr., ed. *The Horn Island Logs of Walter Inglis Anderson.* Memphis, TN: Memphis State University Press, 1973. Reprint, Jackson, MS: University Press of Mississippi, 1985/1991.

Little Room, 1951–1953. Oil on wood

Text copyright © 2009 by Hester Bass. Illustrations copyright © 2009 by E. B. Lewis. The author and publisher acknowledge with gratitude the Family of Walter Inglis Anderson — Mary, Bill, Leif, and John — for copyright permission to reproduce his work, and the Walter Anderson Museum of Art for assistance in securing the images. All images in the Author's Note are used by permission of the Walter Anderson Museum of Art, with the following exceptions: *Thumbelina* used by permission of the Family of Walter Inglis Anderson; *Ocean Springs Community Center* detail photo copyright © Richard Sexton, used by permission of Richard Sexton; *Horn Island* photo copyright © Kevin Berne, used by permission of Kevin Berne; *Little Room* photo copyright © Kevin Berne, used by permission of Kevin Berne.

First edition in this format 2014. Library of Congress Catalog Card Number 2008029674. ISBN 978-0-7636-3583-1 (hardcover). ISBN 978-0-7636-7116-7 (reformatted hardcover). ISBN 978-0-7636-7117-4 (reformatted paperback). This book was typeset in Dante. The illustrations were done in watercolor. Candlewick Press, 99 Dover Street, Somerville, Massachusetts 02144. visit us at www.candlewick.com.
Printed in Dongguan, Guangdong, China.19 TLF 10 9 8 7 6 5

INDEX

Page numbers in *italic* type indicate images.

Anderson, Mac, 32, 37

Anderson, Peter, 32, 37

Anderson, Walter

   art studies, 32

   death, 24, 35

   family background, 31–32

   hat, 4–5, 21, 35

   illnesses, 24, 33

   journals (logs), 18, 35

   locked little room, 7, 24–25, 35, 39

   secret world (*see* Horn Island)

   types of art, 26, 31, 32–35

   wife and children, 7, 33, 34

Bass, Clayton, 37

Best-Maugard, 32

Blue Jays (watercolor), *37*

Chesty Horse (ceramic), *33*

Cottage (watercolor), *34*

Cresson scholarship, 32

Grinstead, Agnes (Sissy), *33, 34, 35*

Gulf Coast, 8, 26, 34, 35, 37

Gulf Island National Seashore, 37

Horn Island, 7, 8, 10–23, 26, 28, 30–31, 35, 37

Horn Island (watercolor), *37*

Hurricane Betsy, 35

Hurricane Katrina, 36

Lion (charcoal), *32*

Mississippi, 1, 8, 32

HESTER BASS is the author of the picture books *So Many Houses*, illustrated by Alik Arzoumanian, and *Seeds of Freedom: The Peaceful Integration of Huntsville, Alabama*, illustrated by E. B. Lewis. About *The Secret World of Walter Anderson*, she says, "It seems to me that Walter Anderson was one of those rare individuals who is fully awake to the world. I find his art and writings, like nature itself, endlessly refreshing. I was once asked what was the one story that I most wanted to publish. This is it." Hester Bass lives in New Mexico.

E. B. LEWIS is the illustrator of more than fifty books for children, including *Seeds of Freedom: The Peaceful Integration of Huntsville, Alabama*, written by Hester Bass. Among his many honors are a Coretta Scott King Medal for *Talkin' About Bessie: The Story of Aviator Elizabeth Coleman* by Nikki Grimes and four Coretta Scott King Honor Books. He says, "'What was has always been. What is has always been. And what will be has always been. Such is the nature of beginning.' (Louis I. Kahn) For me, that is the essence of art." E. B. Lewis lives in New Jersey.